Miss Bea's Band

Louisa Harding

R O W A N

Can you hear the music livvy,
who do think it could be?

Twinkle Sweater instructions page 28

Here comes the band.
First, Miss Bea and her tambourine.

William follows closely,
he blows his whistle – toot, toot, toot.

'Jingle jangle' goes the triangle
when Miss Bea hits it with a stick.

Jingle Jangle Sweater instructions page 34

Shakey, shakey, shakey,
the red Maracas make a lovely sound !

Red Maracas Jacket instructions page 36

Rat-a-tat-tat, rat-a-tat-tat,
Daniel taps out the beat.

Rat Tat Tat Jacket instructions page 38

Picking-up her drum sticks,
Tess joins in banging on her drum.

flower beat sweater instructions page 40

Shaquille concentrates –
he doesn't want to play a wrong note!

Up and down the Xylophone
Tess makes a twinkling sound.

Strumming his Guitar,
Daniel sings a happy song.

The Blues Slipover instructions page 46

The Knitting Patterns
Information Page

Introduction

The knitwear in 'Miss Bea's Band' has been designed to introduce the knitter to different knitted edging and finishing details. We have explained some of the basic techniques used in the book on page 27, such as different embroidery stitches, more specific finishing details will be on the page with your chosen pattern.

The knitting patterns

Each pattern has a chart and simple written instructions that have been colour coded making the different sizes easier to identify. E.g. if you are knitting age 2–3 years follow the instructions in red where you are given a choice. The patterns are laid out as follows:

Age/Size Diagrams

The ages given and the corresponding diagrams are a guide only. The measurements for each knitted piece are shown in a size diagram at the start of every pattern. As all children vary make sure you choose the right garment size, do this by measuring an item of your child's clothing you like the fit of. Choose the instruction size accordingly. If still unsure, knit a larger size, as children always grow.

Yarn

This indicates the amount of yarn needed to complete the design. All the garments that use more than one shade of yarn will have the amount used for each shade.

Needles

Listed are the suggested knitting needles used to make the garment. The smaller needles are usually used for edgings or ribs, the larger needles for the main body fabric.

Buttons/Zips

This indicates the number of buttons or length of zip needed to fasten the finished garment.

Tension

Tension is the single most important factor when you begin knitting. The fabric tension is written for example as 20 sts x 28 rows to 10cm measured over stocking stitch using 4 mm (US 6) needles. Each pattern is worked out mathematically, if the correct tension is not achieved the garment pieces will not measure the size stated in the diagram.

Before embarking on knitting your garment we recommend you check your tension as follows: Using the needle size given cast on 5–10 more stitches than stated in the tension, and work 5–10 more rows. When you have knitted your tension square lay it on a flat surface, place a rule or tape measure horizontally, count the number of stitches equal to the distance of 10cm. Place the measure vertically and count the number of rows, these should equal the tension given in the pattern. If you have too many stitches to 10cm, try again using a thicker needle, if you have too few stitches to 10cm use a finer needle.

Note: Check your tension regularly as you knit, once you become relaxed and confident with your knitting, your tension can change.

Back

This is the start of your pattern. Following the colour code for your chosen size, you will be instructed how many stitches to cast on and to work from chart and written instructions as follows:

Knitting from charts

Each square on a chart represents one stitch; each line of squares indicates a row of knitting. When working from the chart, read odd numbered rows (right side of fabric) from right to left and even numbered rows (wrong side of fabric) from left to right.

Each separate colour used is given a letter and on some charts a corresponding symbol. The different stitches used are also represented by a symbol, e.g. knit and purl, a key to each symbol is with each chart.

Front (Fronts) and Sleeves

The pattern continues with instructions to make these garment pieces.

Pressing

Once you have finished knitting all the pieces it is important that all pieces are pressed, see page 48 for more details.

Neckband (Front bands)

This instruction tells you how to work any finishing off needed to complete your garment, such as knitting a neckband on a sweater or edgings on a cardigan. Once you have completed all the knitting you can begin to make up your garment, see page 48 for making up instructions.

Abbreviations

In the pattern you will find some of the most common words used have been abbreviated:

K	knit
P	purl
st(s)	stitches
inc	increase(e)(ing) knit into the front and back of next st to make 2 stitches.
dec	decreas(e)(ing)
st st	stocking stitch (right side row knit, wrong side row purl)
garter st	garter stitch (knit every row)
beg	begin(ning)
foll	follow(ing)
rem	remain(ing)
rev	reverse(ing)
rep	repeat
alt	alternate
cont	continue
patt	pattern
tog	together
cm	centimetres
in(s)	inch(es)
RS	right side
WS	wrong side
K2tog	knit two sts together to make one stitch
tbl	through back of loop
yo	yarn over, bring yarn over needle before working next st to create an extra loop.
Sl1	slip 1 stitch
psso	pass slip stich over
SSK	slip next 2 sts singly knitwise, and knit together through back of loop

Knitting Techniques
A simple learn to knit guide

Introduction

Using illustrations and simple written instructions we have put together a beginners guide to knitting. With a basic knowledge of the simplest stitches you can create your own unique handknitted garments.

When you begin to knit you feel very clumsy, all fingers and thumbs. This stage passes as confidence and experience grows. Many people are put off hand knitting thinking that they are not using the correct techniques of holding needles, yarn or working of stitches, all knitters develop their own style, so please persevere.

Casting On

This is the term used for making a row of stitches; the foundation row for each piece of knitting. Make a slip knot. Slip this onto a needle. This is the basis of the two casting on techniques as shown below.

Thumb Cast On

This method uses only one needle and gives a neat, but elastic edge. Make a slip knot 1 metre from the cut end of the yarn, you use this length to cast on the stitches. For a knitted piece, the length between cut end and slip knot can be difficult to judge, allow approx 3 times the width measurement.

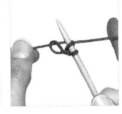

1. Make a slip knot approx 1 metre from the end of the yarn, with ball of yarn to your right.

2. Hold needle in RH. With the cut end of yarn held in LH, wrap yarn around your thumb from left to right anti-clockwise to front.

3. Insert RH needle into yarn around thumb, take yarn attached to ball around the back of RH needle to front.

4. Draw through needle to make a loop.

5. Pull on both ends of yarn gently. Creating a stitch on right hand needle.

6. Repeat from 2. until the required number of stitches has been cast on.

Cable Cast On

This method uses two needles; it gives a firm neat finish. It is important that you achieve an even cast on, this may require practice.

1. With slip knot on LH needle, insert RH needle. Take yarn behind RH needle; bring yarn forward between needles.

2. Draw the RH needle back through the slip knot, making a loop on RH needle with yarn.

3. Slip this loop onto left hand needle; taking care not to pull the loop too tight.

4. Insert the RH needle between the two loops on LH needle. Take yarn behind RH needle; bring forward, between needles.

5. Draw through the RH needle making a loop as before. Slip this stitch onto LH needle.

6. Repeat from 4 until the required number of stitches has been cast on.

How to Knit - The knit stitch is the simplest to learn. By knitting every row you create garter stitch and the simplest of all knitted fabrics.

 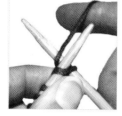  

1. Hold the needle with the cast-on stitches in LH. Insert RH needle into first stitch.

2. Take yarn around the back of RH needle, bring yarn forward between needles.

3. Draw the RH needle through the stitch. Drop loop on LH needle

4. Making a loop on RH needle with yarn. One stitch made.

5. Repeat to the end of the row.

How to Purl - The purl stitch is a little more complicated to master. Using a combination of knit and purl stitches together forms the bases of most knitted fabrics. The most common fabric knitted is stocking stitch, this is created when you knit 1 row, then purl 1 row.

1. Hold the needle with stitches on in LH and with yarn at the front of work, insert RH needle into front of stitch.

2. Take yarn around the back of RH needle, bring yarn to front.

3. Draw the needle through from front to back, making a loop on RH needle.

4. Slip the stitch onto right hand needle. Drop loop on LH needle.

5. Repeat to the end of the row.

Joining in a new yarn - A new ball of yarn can be joined in on either a right side or a wrong side row, but to give a neat finish it is important you do this at the start of a row. Simply drop the old yarn, start knitting with the new ball, then after a few stitches tie the two ends together in a temporary knot. These ends are then sewn into the knitting at the making up stage, see page 48.

Casting Off - This is the method of securing stitches at the top of your knitted fabric. It is important that the cast off edge should be elastic like the rest of the fabric; if you find that your cast off is too tight, try using a larger needle. You can cast off knitwise (as illustrated), purlwise, or in a combination of stitches, such as rib.

1. Hold the needle with the stitches on in LH, knit the first stitch.

2. Knit the next stitch from LH needle, two stitches on RH needle.

3. Using the point of LH needle; insert into first stitch on RH needle.

4. Take the first stitch over the second stitch.

5. One stitch on right hand needle.

6. Rep from 2 until one stitch on RH needle. Cut yarn, draw cut end through last stitch to secure.

itting details and finishing touches

his book we have looked at different ways of adding
rest to your knitting; the techniques used are
lained here design by design.

jinkle Sweater

s garment has a fringe and beads, which are sewn
once the garment is completed. To make the

fringing: for each
tassel cut 4 x
15 cm lengths,
fold the strands
in half and draw
the folded end
through the eyelet
in the sweaters
hem, draw the
loose ends of yarn
ough the loop, and pull firmly to form a knot. Trim
ends once the fringe is complete.
ish the sweater by sewing in a bead into every
er stitch on row 4 of the body and sleeve hems as
stration shows.

ng-a-ling Cardigan

s garment has a contrasting colour frill edging, this
achieved by casting on a large number of stitches
d then decreasing them to create a pattern, leaving
correct stitches needed for the with of garment
ly, this creates the frill.

ee Willie Whistle Sweater

s sweater has a Kangaroo pocket, which is knitted
he same time as the sweater front, to emphasise the
cket we have knitted it in a contrast colour.

ngle Jangle Sweater

s sweater has a lace textured flower border. This
achieved by working a lace stitch pattern, produced

by using the
eyelet method of
increasing. These
are usually worked
in conjunction with
a decrease so
that the number of
stitches remains
constant at the
d of each row. The pattern in this sweater, however,
achieved by increasing stitches on some rows and
creasing them on subsequent rows. This is quite a
mplex pattern to work, the effect is very rewarding.

Red Maracas Jacket

Both textured knitting and embroidery are used to
create interest on this jacket. Textured diamonds

are knitted into
the jacket fronts,
which are then
embroidered
using oddments
of yarn and Lazy
Daisy stitch, this
is a method of
working individual
chain stitches to
form petals which
can be grouped
together to make
a flower of 4 or 5 petals, or singly to create a leaf.

Rat Tat Tat Jacket

Interest is added to this very simple jacket by working
blanket stitch around the garment's edges using a

contrasting colour
yarn as illustrated,
a very effective
way of finishing off
a design.

Flower Beat Sweater

Adding pretty knitted flowers (as illustrated) enhances
this plain sweater. These are knitted using oddments
of yarn and then sewn on and secured into place with

a button; you
can add as many
flowers as you like.

Ribbon Melody Cardigan

A thin ribbon is threaded through the eyelet pattern
around the edges of this pretty cardigan. We also
made small bows and stitched these into place at the
centre of the sleeves.

Plink Plonk Sweater

We have made two twisted cords to thread through this
sweaters turned up hem and laced up neck edging.

Each twisted cord
is made as folls:
Cut 3 x 3 metre
lengths of yarn.
Knot the strands
together at each
end. Attach one
end to a hook or door handle, insert a knitting needle
through the other end. Twist the needle - the tighter
the twisting, the firmer the finished cord will be. Hold
the cord in the centre with one hand (you may need
some help); bring both ends of cord together, allowing
the two halves to twist together. Keep the cord straight
and avoid tangling. Knot the cut ends together and
trim. Once you have threaded the cords through the
hem and neck, adjust to required length.

The Blues Slipover

Swiss darning (duplicate stitch) makes this simple
intarsia block slipover look more complicated than it is.

Swiss darning is a
form of embroidery
that duplicates the
knitted stitches
so that it looks as
if the design has
been knitted in.
**Swiss darning
horizontally:**
Work from left to
right. Thread a
blunt needle with embroidery yarn, *bring the needle
out at the base of the first stitch, take it around the
top of the stitch under the stitch above, then insert
the needle back through the base of the same stitch*,
covering the original stitch completely, repeat this into
every stitch along the row.
Swiss darning vertically: Work from bottom to top.
Work as above from * to *, work into every alternate
horizontal stitch to make a vertical line as illustrated.

Twinkle Sweater

Age 1-2 years 2-3 years 3-4 years

Size

Back

Front

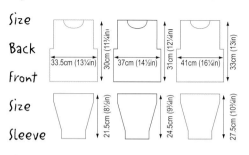

33.5cm (13¼in) 30cm (11¾in) 37cm (14½in) 31cm (12¼in) 41cm (16¼in) 33cm (13in)

Size

Sleeve

21.5cm (8½in) 24.5cm (9¾in) 27.5cm (10¾in)

Yarn
Rowan All Seasons Cotton x 50g balls
Blackcurrant   5   6   6

Needles
1 pair 4 mm (US 6) needles for edging
1 pair 5 mm (US 8) needles for main body

Beads approx 135 clear glass beads

Tension
17 sts and 24 rows to 10 cm measured over stocking
stitch using 5 mm (US 8) needles

Back
Using 4 mm (US 6) needles cast on 57,63,69 sts and
work from chart and written instructions as folls:
Chart row 1: Knit.
Chart row 2: Knit.
Chart row 3: K4,1,4(yo, K2tog, K4) 8,10,10 times, yo
K2tog, K3,0,3.
Chart row 4: Knit.
Chart row 5: K1,0,1(P1, K1) to last 0,1,0 st, P0,1,0.
Chart row 6: K1,0,1(P1, K1) to last 0,1,0 st, P0,1,0.

Cont in moss st until chart row 10 completed.
Change to 5 mm (US 8) needles and work in stocking
stitch only as on chart.
Chart row 11: Knit.
Chart row 12: Purl.
Work until chart row 42,42,46 completed.
Shape armhole
Cast off 5 sts at the beg next 2 rows. (47,53,59 sts)
Work until chart row 74,76,82 completed.
Shape shoulders and back neck
Cast off 3,4,5 sts at beg next 2 rows.
Chart row 77,79,85: Cast off 3,4,5 sts, knit until 7 sts
on RH needle, turn and leave rem sts on a holder.
Chart row 78,80,86: Cast off 3 sts, purl to end.
Cast off rem 4 sts.
Slip centre 21,23,25 sts onto a holder, rejoin yarn to
rem sts and knit to end. (10,11,12 sts)
Chart row 78,80,86: Cast off 3,4,5 sts, purl to end.
Chart row 79,81,87: Cast off 3 sts, knit to end.
Cast off rem 4 sts.

Front
Work as for back until chart row 70,72,78 completed.
Shape front neck
Chart row 71,73,79: Knit 16,18,20 sts, turn and leave
rem sts on a holder.
Chart row 72,74,80: Cast off 4 sts, purl to end.
Dec 1 st at neck edge on next 2 rows. (10,12,14 sts)
Shape shoulder
Cast off 3,4,5 sts at beg next row and foll alt row.
Work 1 row.
Cast off rem 4 sts.
Slip centre 15,17,19 sts onto a holder, rejoin yarn to rem
sts and knit to end. (16,18,20 sts)
Chart row 72,74,80: Purl 1 row.
Chart row 73,75,81: Cast off 4 sts, knit to end.
Dec 1 st at neck edge on next 2 rows. (10,12,14 sts)
Shape shoulder
Cast off 3,4,5 sts at beg next row and foll alt row.
Work 1 row.
Cast off rem 4 sts.

Sleeves (both alike)
Using 4 mm (US 6) needles cast on 29,31,33 sts work
from written instructions as folls:
Row 1: Knit.
Row 2: Knit.
Rept these 2 rows once more
Now working from chart, work in moss st as folls:
Chart row 5: K1,0,1(P1, K1) to last 0,1,0 st, P0,1,0.
Chart row 6: K1,0,1(P1, K1) to last 0,1,0 st, P0,1,0.
Cont in moss st until chart row 10 completed.

Change to 5mm (US 8) needles and work in stockin
stitch only as on chart.
Chart row 11: Inc into first st, knit to last st, inc into
last st. (31,33,35 sts)
Chart row 12: Purl.
Cont from chart, shaping sides by inc as indicated to
45,47,51 sts.
Work without further shaping until chart row 54,60,6
completed. Cast off.

Press all pieces as instructed on 48.

Neckband
Join right shoulder using backstitch.
Using 4mm (US 6) needles pick up and knit 10 sts
down left front neck, knit across 15,17,19 sts on hold
pick up and knit 10 sts to shoulder and 3 sts down
right back neck, knit across 21,23,25 sts on holder
and pick up and knit 3 sts to shoulder. (62,66,70 sts
Edging row 1 (WS): K1,P1 to end.
Edging row 2: P1,K1 to end.
Work 3 more rows in moss stitch.
Knit 3 rows ending with a RS row.
Cast off knitwise.
Join left shoulder and neck edging using back stitch.

Complete sweater as instructed on page 48.
Add fringing and sew on beads as photo, see page 2

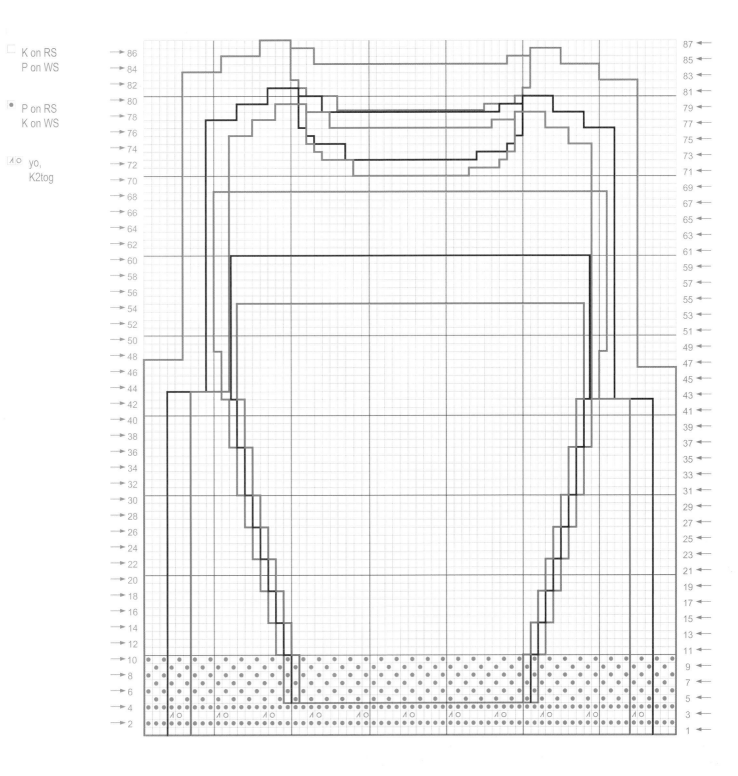

K on RS
P on WS

P on RS
K on WS

∧o yo,
K2tog

29

Ting-a-ling Cardigan

Age 1-2 years   2-3 years   3-4 years

Size

Back

Front

Size

Sleeve

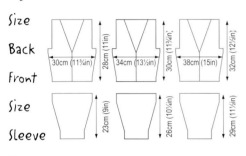

Yarn
Rowan Handknit Cotton x 50g balls

A. Purple	4	4	5
B. Pink	2	2	2

Needles
1 pair 3 ¼ mm (US 3) needles for edging
1 pair 4 mm (US 6) needles for main body

Buttons 5 (small)

Tension
20 sts and 28 rows to 10 cm measured over stocking stitch using 4 mm (US 6) needles

Back
Using 3 ¼ mm (US 3) needles and yarn B, cast on 125,145,165 sts and work edging from written instructions as folls:
Row 1: Knit.
Row 2: Knit.
Row 3: K1, (P1, K1,P1, K7) 12,14,16 times, (P1, K1) twice.
Row 4: K1, P1, (K1, P9) 12,14,16 times, K1, P1, K1.

Row 5: as row 3.
Row 6: as row 4.
Row 7(dec): K1, (P1, K1,P1, SSK, K3, K2 tog) 12,14,16 times, (P1, K1) twice. (101,117,133 sts)
Row 8: K1, P1, (K1, P7) 12,14,16 times, K1, P1, K1.
Row 9(dec): K1, (P1, K1,P1, SSK, K2 tog) 12,14,16 times, (P1, K1) twice. (77,89,101 sts)
Row 10: K1, P1, (K1, P5) 12,14,16 times, K1, P1, K1.
Row 11(dec): K1, (P1, K1,P1, slip 1, K2tog, psso) 12,14,16 times, (P1, K1) twice. (53,61,69 sts)
Row 12: K1, P1, (K1, P3) 12,14,16 times, K1, P1, K1.
Row 13: (K1, P1) to last st, K1.
Row 14: as row 12.
Row 15: as row 13.
Row 16: as row 12.
Change to 4 mm (US 6) needles and yarn A, beg with a K row cont in st st working from chart until chart row 4 completed.
Chart row 5: Inc into first st, knit to last st, inc into last st. (55,63,71 sts)
Cont from chart shaping sides by inc as indicated to 61,69,77 sts.
Work without further shaping until chart row 28,30,34 completed.
Shape armhole
Cast off 6 sts at the beg next 2 rows.
(49,57,65 sts)
Work until chart row 64,70,76 completed.
Shape shoulders and back neck
Cast off 4,5,6 sts at the beg next 2 rows.
Chart row 67,73,79: Cast off 4,5,6 sts, knit until 7,8,9 sts on RH needle, turn and leave rem sts on a holder.
Chart row 68,74,80: Cast off 3 sts, purl to end.
Cast off rem 4,5,6 sts.
Rejoin yarn and cast off centre 19,21,23 sts, knit to end. (11,13,15 sts)
Chart row 68,74,80: Cast off 4,5,6 sts, purl to end. (7,8,9 sts)
Chart row 69,75,81: Cast off 3 sts, knit to end.
Cast off rem 4,5,6 sts.

Left Front
Using 3 ¼ mm (US 3) needles and yarn B, cast on 65,75,85 sts and work from written instructions as folls:
Row 1: Knit.
Row 2: Knit.
Row 3: K1, (P1, K1,P1, K7) 6,7,8 times, (P1, K1) twice.
Row 4: K1, P1, (K1, P9) 6,7,8 times, K1, P1, K1.
Row 5: as row 3.
Row 6: as row 4.
Row 7(dec): K1, (P1, K1,P1, SSK, K3, K2 tog) 6,7,8 times, (P1, K1) twice. (53,61,69 sts)

Row 8: K1, P1, (K1, P7) 6,7,8 times, K1, P1, K1.
Row 9(dec): K1, (P1, K1,P1, SSK, K1, K2 tog) 6,7,8 times, (P1, K1) twice. (41,47,53 sts)
Row 10: K1, P1, (K1, P5) 6,7,8 times, K1, P1, K1.
Row 11(dec): K1, (P1, K1,P1, slip 1, K2tog, psso) 6,7,8 times, (P1, K1) twice. (29,33,37 sts)
Row 12: K1, P1, (K1, P3) 6,7,8 times, K1, P1, K1.
Row 13: (K1, P1) to last st, K1.
Row 14: as row 12.
Row 15: as row 13.
Row 16: as row 12.
Note: 4 sts at centre are worked in moss st througho and are **not** shown on chart.
Change to 4 mm (US 6) needles and yarn A, work in st st with 4 sts of moss st at centre front as folls:
Chart row 1: Knit to last 4 sts, (P1, K1) twice.
Chart row 2: (K1, P1) twice, purl to end.
Chart row 3: as row 1.
Chart row 4: as row 2.
Chart row 5: Inc into first st, patt to end.
(30,34,38 sts)
Cont from chart, shaping side edge by inc as indicate to 33,37,41 sts.
Work without further shaping until chart row 28,30,34 completed.
Shape armhole
Cast off 6 sts at the beg next row, knit 21,25,29 SSK, (P1, K1) twice. (26,30,34 sts)
Work 1 row.
Next row (dec): Knit 20,24,28 SSK, (P1, K1) twice.
(25,29,33 sts)
Work 1 row.
Cont to dec internally at front neck as indicated on chart to 16,19,22 sts.
Work without further shaping until chart row 64,70,76 completed.
Shape shoulder
Cast off 4,5,6 sts at the beg next row and 2 foll alt rows. (4 sts)

Back neck edging
Cont to work on these 4 sts in moss st until edging measures 6,6.5,7cm, cast off.

Right Front
Using 3 ¼ mm (US 3) needles and yarn B, cast on 65,75,85 sts and work edging from written instruction as for left front. (29,33,37 sts)
Note: 4 sts at centre are worked in moss st througho and are **not** shown on chart.
Change to 4mm (US 6) needles and yarn A, work in st st with moss st edging as for left front, foll chart for

ht front and reversing shaping
d working neck decs as K2tog.

eeves (both alike)
ing 3 ¼ mm (US 3) needles
d yarn B, cast on 75,77,79 sts
d work from written instructions
folls:

w 1: Knit.

w 2: Knit.

w 3: K0,0,1, P0,1,1, K1, (P1,
P1, K7) 7 times, (P1, K1) twice,
,1,1, K0,0,1.

w 4: K0,0,1, P0,1,1, K1, P1 (K1,
) 7 times, K1, P1, K1, P0,1,1,
,0,1.

w 5: as row 3.

w 6: as row 4.

w 7(dec): K0,0,1, P0,1,1, K1,
1, K1,P1, SSK, K3, K2 tog)
imes, (P1, K1) twice, P0,1,1,
,0,1.

,63,65 sts)

w 8: K0,0,1, P0,1,1, K1, P1 (K1,
) 7 times, K1, P1, K1, P0,1,1,
,0,1.

w 9(dec): K0,0,1, P0,1,1, K1,
1, K1,P1, SSK, K1, K2 tog)
imes, (P1, K1) twice. P0,1,1,
,0,1.

,49,51 sts)

w 10: K0,0,1, P0,1,1, K1, P1 (K1,
) 7 times, K1, P1, K1, P0,1,1,
,0,1.

w 11(dec): K0,0,1, P0,1,1, K1,
1, K1,P1, slip 1, K2tog, psso)
imes, (P1, K1) twice, P0,1,1,
,0,1.

,35,37 sts)

w 12: K0,0,1, P0,1,1, K1, P1 (K1,
) 7 times, K1, P1, K1, P0,1,1,
,0,1.

w 13: P0,1,0, (K1, P1) to last
,1 st, K1,0,1.

w 14: as row 12.

w 15: as row 13.

w 16: as row 12.

hange to 4 mm (US 6) needles
d yarn A, beg with a K row work
st st only from chart until row 4
mpleted:

hart row 5: Inc into first st, knit

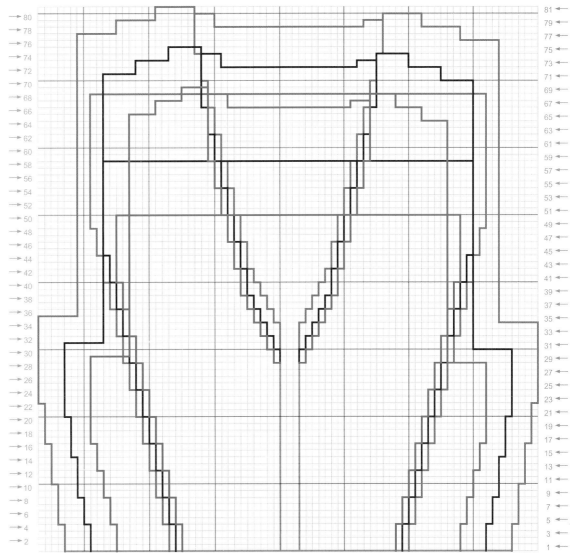

K on RS, P on WS

to last st, inc into last st.
(35,37,39 sts)

Chart row 6: Purl to end.
Cont from chart, shaping sides by inc as indicated to
53,57,61 sts.
Work without further shaping until chart row 50,58,68 completed.
Cast off.

Press all pieces as instructed on page 48.
Join both shoulder seams using backstitch.

Edgings
Slip st edging into place at back neck.
Sew 5 buttons to left front, the first to come 1 cm up from lower
edge, last to come 1 cm down from start of front slope shaping
and rem 3 buttons spaced evenly between.
To fasten buttons, push them through small hole between centre
sts on right front moss st band.

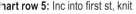

Wee Willie Whistle Sweater

Age 1-2 years 2-3 years 3-4 years

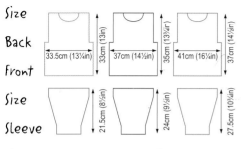

Size

Back

33.5cm (13¼in) 33cm (13in) 37cm (14½in) 35cm (13¾in) 41cm (16¼in) 37cm (14½in)

Front

Size

Sleeve

21.5cm (8½in) 24cm (9½in) 27.5cm (10¾in)

Yarn

Rowan All Seasons Cotton x 50g balls

A. Mocha Choc	4	4	5
B. Cookie	1	1	1

Needles

1 pair 4 mm (US 6) needles for rib
1 pair 5 mm (US 8) needles for main body

OK

Tension

17 sts and 24 rows to 10 cm measured over stocking stitch using 5 mm (US 8) needles

Back

Using 4 mm (US 6) needles and yarn B cast on 57,63,69 sts and work from chart and written instructions as folls:
Chart row 1: K0,3,1 (P2, K3) 11,11,13 times, P2, K0,3,1.
Chart row 2: P0,3,1 (K2, P3) 11,11,13 times, K2, P0,3,1.
Change to yarn A and work in rib as set until chart row 10 completed.
Change to 5 mm (US 8) needles and work in st st from chart until chart row 50,52,54 completed.
Shape armhole

Cast off 5 sts at the beg next 2 rows. (47,53,59 sts)
Work until chart row 80,84,88 completed.
Shape shoulders and back neck
Chart row 81,85,89: Knit 13,15,17 sts, turn and leave rem sts on a holder.
Chart row 82,86,90: Cast off 3 sts, purl to end.
Slip rem 10,12,14 sts onto a holder.
Slip centre 21,23,25 sts onto a holder, rejoin yarn to rem sts and knit to end. (13,15,17 sts)
Work 1 row.
Chart row 83,87,91: Cast off 3 sts, knit to end.
Slip rem 10,12,14 sts onto a holder.

Front

Work as for back until chart row 10 completed. Change to 5 mm (US 8) needles and work pocket as folls:
Chart row 11: K12,15,18, slip next 33 sts onto a spare needle for pocket front, turn and cast on 33 sts using the cable cast on method, turn, and knit rem K12,15,18, sts.
Cont in st st only until chart row 40 completed, leave these sts on a holder.
Work pocket front
Return to sts on holder for pocket front and, with RS facing, join in yarn B.
Work 30 rows for pocket front as on chart using yarn B as folls:
Pocket chart row 1: Knit.
Pocket chart row 2: Purl.
Pocket chart row 3: P4, K25, P4.
Pocket chart row 4: K4, P25, K4.
Pocket chart row 5: Knit.
Pocket chart row 6: Purl.
Rep these 6 rows once more.
Rep rows 1 & 2
Pocket chart row 15(dec): P4, sl1, K1, psso, K21, K2tog, P4.
Pocket chart row 16: K4, P23, K4.
Work 4 rows in st st.
Dec internally as above on next row and foll 6th row. (27 sts) Work straight until chart row 30 completed.
Join in pocket
Placing WS of pocket front in front of sweater front work as folls:
Chart row 40: Using yarn A K15,18,21 sts from sweater front, place sts from pocket in front of sweater front and knit the next 27 sts together, knit to end. (57,63,69 sts)
Cont to work as for back until row 74,78,82 completed.
Shape front neck
Chart row 75,79,83: Knit 16,18,20 sts, turn and leave rem sts on a holder.

Chart row 76,80,84: Cast off 4 sts, purl to end.
Dec 1 st at neck edge on next 2 rows. (10,12,14 sts)
Work without further shaping until chart row 82,86,90 completed.
Slip rem sts onto a holder.
Slip centre 15,17,19 sts onto a holder, rejoin yarn to rem sts and knit to end. (16,18,20 sts)
Work 1 row.
Chart row 77,81,85: Cast off 4 sts, knit to end.
Dec 1 st at neck edge on next 2 rows. (10,12,14 sts)
Work without further shaping until chart row 83,87,91 completed. Slip rem sts onto a holder.

Sleeves (both alike)

Using 4 mm (US 6) needles and yarn B cast on 29,31,33 sts and work from chart and written instructions as folls:
Chart row 1: K1,2,3 (P2, K3) 5 times, P2, K1,2,3.
Chart row 2: P1,2,3 (K2, P3) 5 times, K2, P1,2,3.
Change to yarn A and work in rib as set until chart row 10 completed.
Change to 5 mm (US 8) needles and work in st st only from chart as folls:
Chart row 11: Inc into first st, knit to last st, inc into last st. (31,33,35 sts)
Chart row 12: Purl.
Cont from chart shaping sides by inc as indicated to 45,47,51 sts.
Work without further shaping until chart row 54,60,68 completed. Cast off.

Press all pieces as instructed on page 48.

Neckband

Using yarn A join right shoulder seam by knitting sts together on the RS of garment as shown on page 48.
Using 4 mm (US 6) needles pick up and knit 10 sts down left front neck, knit across 15,17,19 sts on holder, pick up and knit 10 sts to shoulder and 3 sts down right back neck, knit across 21,23,25 sts on holder and pick up and knit 3 sts to shoulder. (62,66,70 sts)
Rib row 1(WS): K1,0,0 (K2, P3) 12,13,14 times, K1,1,
Rib row 2: P1,1,0 (K3, P2) 12,13,14 times, P1,0,0.
Work these 2 rows twice more.
Change to yarn B and work 2 rows in rib as set.
Cast off in rib.
Join left shoulder seam by knitting sts together on the RS of garment as above using yarn A.
Join neckband seam using backstitch.
Join cast on edge of pocket to top of rib for sweater behind pocket front.
Complete sweater as instructed on page 48.

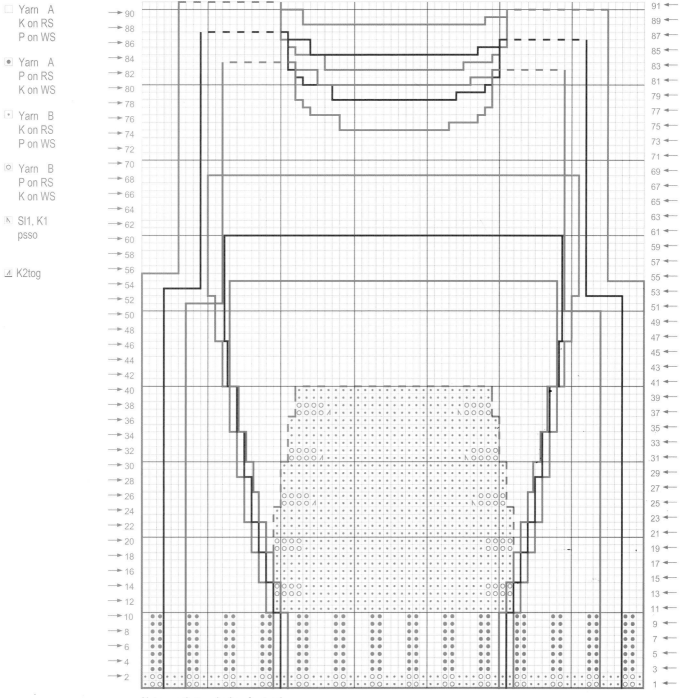

Yarn A
K on RS
P on WS

Yarn A
P on RS
K on WS

Yarn B
K on RS
P on WS

Yarn B
P on RS
K on WS

Sl1, K1
psso

K2tog

Note - pocket worked on front only

33

Jingle Jangle Sweater

Age 1-2 years   2-3 years   3-4 years

Size

Back

Front

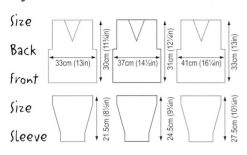

Size

Sleeve

Yarn
Rowan Wool Cotton x 50g balls
Lilac   4   5   5

Needles
1 pair 3 ¼ mm (US 3) needles for edging
1 pair 3 ¾ mm (US 5) needles for lace border
1 pair 4 mm (US 6) needles for main body

Tension
22 sts and 30 rows to 10 cm measured over stocking stitch using 4 mm (US 6) needles

Back
Using 3 ¾ mm (US 5) needles cast on 75,83,91 sts and work flower border from written instructions as folls:
Row 1: Knit.
Row 2: Knit.
Row 3: Knit.
Row 4: K13,17,21, (P1, K23) twice,P1, K13,17,21.
Row 5: K11,15,19, (K2tog, yo, K1,yo, SSK, K19) twice, K2tog, yo, K1,yo, SSK, K11,15,19.
Row 6: K11,15,19, (P5, K19) twice, P5, K11,15,19.
Row 7: K10,14,18 (K2tog, yo, K3,yo, SSK, K17) twice,

K2tog, yo, K3,yo, SSK, K10,14,18.
Row 8: K10,14,18 (P7, K17) twice, P7, K10,14,18.
Row 9: K9,13,17 [(K2tog, yo) twice, K1, (yo, SSK) twice, K15] twice, (K2tog, yo) twice, K1, (yo, SSK) twice, K9,13,17.
Row 10: K9,13,17 (P9, K15) twice, P9, K9,13,17.
Row 11: K8,12,16 [(K2tog, yo) twice, K3, (yo, SSK) twice, K13] twice, (K2tog, yo) twice, K3, (yo, SSK) twice, K8,12,16.
Row 12: K8,12,16 (P4, K1, P1, K1, P4, K13) twice, P4, K1, P1, K1, P4, K8,12,16.
Row 13: K7,11,15 [(K2tog, yo) twice, K5, (yo, SSK) twice, K11] twice (K2tog, yo) twice, K5, (yo, SSK) twice, K7,11,15.
Row 14: K7,11,15 (P4, K2, P1, K2, P4, K11) twice, P4, K2, P1, K2, P4, K7,11,15.
Row 15: K6,10,14 [(K2tog, yo) twice, K3, yo, K1, yo, K3 (yo, SSK) twice, K9] twice, (K2tog, yo) twice, K3, yo, K1, yo, K3 (yo, SSK) twice, K6,10,14. (81,89,97 sts)
Row 16: K6,10,14 (P4, K3, P3, K3, P4, K9) twice, P4, K3, P3, K3, P4, K6,10,14.
Row 17: K5,9,13 [(K2tog, yo) twice, K5, yo, K1, yo, K5 (yo, SSK) twice, K7] twice, (K2tog, yo) twice, K5, yo, K1, yo, K5 (yo, SSK) twice, K5,9,13. (87,95,103 sts)
Row 18: K5,9,13 (P4, K4, P5, K4, P4, K7) twice, P4, K4, P5, K4, P4, K5,9,13.
Row 19: K4,8,12 [(K2tog, yo) twice, K7, yo, K1, yo, K7 (yo, SSK) twice, K5] twice, (K2tog, yo) twice, K7, yo, K1, yo, K7 (yo, SSK) twice, K4,8,12. (93,101,109 sts)
Row 20: K4,8,12 (P4, K5, P7, K5, P4, K5) twice, P4, K5, P7, K5, P4, K4,8,12.
Row 21: K3,7,11 [(K2tog, yo) twice, K9, yo, K1, yo, K9 (yo, SSK) twice, K3] twice, (K2tog, yo) twice, K9, yo, K1, yo, K9 (yo, SSK) twice, K3,7,11. (99,107,115 sts)
Row 22: K3,7,11 (P4, K6, P9, K6, P4, K3) twice, P4, K6, P9, K6, P4, K3,7,11.
Row 23: K2,6,10 [(K2tog, yo) twice, K7, SSK, K5, K2tog, K7 (yo, SSK) twice, K1] twice, (K2tog, yo) twice, K7, SSK, K5, K2tog, K7 (yo, SSK) twice, K2,6,10. (93,101,109 sts)
Row 24: K2,6,10 (P4, K7, P7, K7, P4, K1) twice, P4, K7, P7, K7, P4, K2,6,10.
Row 25: K13,17,21 (SSK, K3, K2tog, K23) twice, SSK, K3, K2tog, K13,17,21. (87,95,103 sts)
Row 26: K13,17,21 (P5, K23) twice, P5, K13,17,21.
Row 27: K13,17,21 (SSK, K1, K2tog, K23) twice, SSK, K1, K2tog, K13,17,21. (81,89,97 sts)
Row 28: K13,17,21 (P3, K23) twice, P3, K13,17,21.
Row 29: K13,17,21 (sl1, K2tog, psso, K23) twice, sl1, K2tog, psso, K13,17,21. (75,83,91 sts)
Row 30: As row 4.
Change to 4 mm (US 6) needles and work 4 more rows

in garter st.
Cont to work in st st only from chart until row 26,28,3☐ completed.
Shape armhole
Cast off 6 sts at the beg next 2 rows. (63,71,79 sts)
Work until chart row 66,70,76 completed.
Shape shoulders and back neck
Cast off 6,7,8 sts at the beg next 2 rows.
Chart row 69,73,79: Cast off 6,7,8 sts, knit until 8,9,1☐ sts on RH needle, turn and leave rem sts on a holder.
Chart row 70,74,80: Cast off 3 sts, purl to end.
Cast off rem 5,6,7 sts.
Slip centre 23,25,27 sts onto a holder, rejoin yarn to rem sts and knit to end. (14,16,18 sts)
Chart row 70,74,80: Cast off 6,7,8 sts, purl to end. (8,9,10 sts)
Chart row 71,75,81: Cast off 3 sts, knit to end.
Cast off rem 5,6,7 sts.

Front
Work as for back until chart row 36,38,42 completed.
Shape front neck
Chart row 37,39,43: Knit 31,35,39 sts, turn and leave rem sts on a holder.
Work 1 row.
Chart row 39,41,45: Knit to last 2 sts, SSK.
Work 1 row.
Cont to dec as indicated at front neck until 17,20,23 st☐ rem.
Work until chart row 66,70,76 completed.
Shape shoulder
Cast off 6,7,8 sts at beg next row and foll alt row.
Work 1 row.
Cast off rem 5,6,7 sts.
Slip centre st onto a holder, rejoin yarn to rem sts and knit to end. (31,35,39 sts)
Work 1 row.
Chart row 39,41,45: K2tog, knit to end.
Work 1 row.
Cont to dec as indicated at front neck until 17,20,23 st☐ rem.
Work until chart row 67,71,77 completed.
Shape shoulder
Cast off 6,7,8 sts at beg next row and foll alt row.
Work 1 row. Cast off rem 5,6,7 sts.

Sleeves (both alike)
Using 3 ¼ mm (US 3) needles cast on 39,41,43 sts an☐ work from written instructions as folls:
Row 1: Knit.
Row 2: Knit.
Cont in garter st from chart until row 10 completed

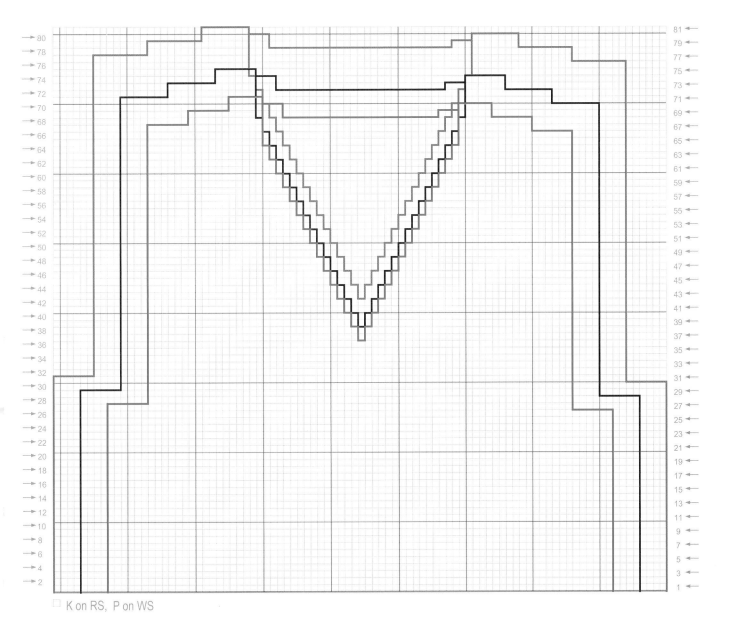

K on RS, P on WS

hange to 4 mm (US 6) needles.
ow 11: Inc into first st, knit to last st, inc into last st.
1,43,45 sts)
ow 12: Purl.
Work 2 rows in st st.
ont in st st and **at the same time** shape sides by
c at both ends of next row and every foll 4th row to
7,49,51 sts then every foll 6th row to 57,61,65 sts.
Work without further shaping until 66,76,86 rows

completed. Cast off.
Press all pieces as instructed on page 48.

Neckband
Join right shoulder seam using backstitch.
Using 3 ¼ mm (US 3) needles pick up and knit
26,27,28 sts down left front neck, knit across 1st on
holder, pick up and knit 26,27,28 sts to shoulder and 3
sts down right back neck, knit across 23,25,27 sts on

holder, pick up and knit 3 sts to shoulder. (82,86,90 sts)
Edging row 1 (WS row): K53,56,59, SSK, K1,K2tog,
K24,25,26.
Edging row 2 (RS row): Knit.
Cast off 52,55,58 sts, SSK, cast off,K1, cast off, K2tog,
cast off rem sts.
Join left shoulder seam and neckband using backstitch.
Complete sweater as instructed in making up
instructions on page 48.

Red Maracas Jacket

Age 1-2 years 2-3 years 3-4 years

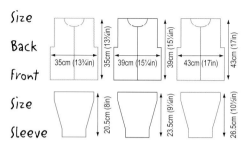

Size
Back
Front

35cm (13¾in) 35cm (13¾in) 39cm (15¼in) 43cm (17in) 43cm (17in)

Size
Sleeve

20.5cm (8in) 23.5cm (9¼in) 26.5cm (10½in)

Yarn
Rowan Handknit Cotton x 50g balls
Spanish Red   7   8   8
Oddments of yarn for embroidery

Needles
1 pair 3 ¼ mm (US 3) needles for edging
1 pair 4 mm (US 6) needles for main body

Buttons 7

Tension
20 sts and 28 rows to 10 cm measured over stocking
stitch using 4 mm (US 6) needles

Note The chart is for the jacket fronts only, work from
written instructions for back and sleeves, using chart
as a guide for back as shaping and rows are the same.

Back
Using 3 ¼ mm (US 3) needles cast on 71,79,87 sts and
work from written instructions as folls:
Row 1: K1,0,0, P3,2,0, (K3, P3) 11,12,14 times, K1,3,3,
P0,2,0.

Row 2: P1,0,0, K3,2,0, (P3, K3) 11,12,14 times, P1,3,3,
K0,2,0.
Row 3: As row 1.
Row 4: K1,0,0, P3,2,0, (K3, P3) 11,12,14 times, K1,3,3,
P0,2,0.
Row 5: P1,0,0, K3,2,0, (P3, K3) 11,12,14 times, P1,3,3,
K0,2,0.
Row 6: As row 4.
Work as patt set until chart row 12 completed.
Change to 4 mm (US 6) needles, work in st st only
until row 60,70,78 completed.
Shape armhole
Cast off 6 sts at the beg next 2 rows. (59,67,75 sts)
Cont until chart row 100,112,122 completed.
Shape shoulders and back neck
Cast off 5,6,7 sts at the beg next 2 rows.
Row 103,115,125: Cast off 5,6,7 sts, knit until 9,10,11
sts on RH needle, turn and leave rem sts on
a holder.
Row 104,116,126: Cast off 3 sts, purl to end.
Cast off rem 6,7,8 sts.
Rejoin yarn to rem sts, cast off centre 21,23,25 sts,
knit to end. (14,16,18 sts)
Row 104,116,126: Cast off 5,6,7 sts, purl to end.
(9,10,11 sts)
Row 105,117,127: Cast off 3 sts, knit to end.
Cast off rem 6,7,8 sts.

Left Front
Using 3 ¼ mm (US 3) needles cast on 33,37,41 sts and
work from written instructions as folls:
Chart row 1: K1,0,0, P3,2,0, (K3, P3) 4,5,6 times, K3, P2.
Chart row 2: K2, P3, (K3, P3) 4,5,6 times, K3,2,0,
P1,0,0.
Chart row 3: As row 1.
Chart row 4: P2, K3, (P3, K3) 4,5,6 times, P3,2,0,
K1,0,0.
Chart row 5: P1,0,0, K3,2,0, (P3, K3) 4,5,6 times, P3, K2.
Chart row 6: As row 4.
Work as patt set until chart row 12 completed.
Change to 4 mm (US 6) needles cont to work from
chart working in patt st st only as indicated until chart
row 60,70,78 completed.
Shape armhole
Cast off 6 sts at the beg next row. (27,31,35 sts)
Cont until chart row 93,105,115 completed.
Shape front neck
Chart row 94,106,116: Cast off 5,6,7 sts, patt to end.
(22,25,28 sts)
Work 1 row.
Chart row 96,108,118: Cast off 4 sts, patt to end.
Dec 1 st at neck edge on next 2 rows. (16,19,22 sts)

Shape shoulder
Cast off 5,6,7 sts at beg next and foll alt row.
Work 1 row.
Cast off rem 6,7,8 sts.

Right Front
Using 3 ¼ mm (US 3) needles cast on 33,37,41 sts and
work from chart and written instructions as folls:
Chart row 1: P2, K3, (P3, K3) 4,5,6 times, P3,2,0,
K1,0,0.
Chart row 2: P1,0,0, K3,2,0, (P3, K3) 4,5,6 times, P3,
K2.
Chart row 3: As row 1.
Chart row 4: K1,0,0, P3,2,0, (K3, P3) 4,5,6 times, K3,
P2.
Chart row 5: K2, P3, (K3, P3) 4,5,6 times, K3,2,0,
P1,0,0.
Chart row 6: As row 4.
Work until chart row 12 completed.
Change to 4 mm (US 6) needles and work in patt st st
from chart. Complete to match left front, foll chart for
right front and reversing all shaping.

Sleeves (both alike)
Using 3 ¼ mm (US 3) needles cast on 35,37,39 sts and
work from written instructions as folls:
Row 1: K1,2,3, (P3, K3) 5 times, P3, K1,2,3.
Row 2: P1,2,3, (K3, P3) 5 times, K3, P1,2,3.
Row 3: As row 1.
Row 4: K1,2,3, (P3, K3) 5 times, P3, K1,2,3.
Row 5: P1,2,3, (K3, P3) 5 times, K3, P1,2,3.
Row 6: As row 4.
Work as patt set until 12 rows in all completed.
Change to 4 mm (US 6) needles.
Row 13: Inc into first st, knit to last st, inc into last st.
(37,39,41 sts)
Row 14: Purl.
Work 2 rows in st st.
Inc 1 st at either end next row and every foll 4th row to
55,59,63 sts.
Work without further shaping until 60,68,76 row.
Cast off.

Press all pieces as instructed on page 48.

Button band
With RS of left front facing and using 3 ¼ mm (US 3)
needles pick up and knit 69,75,81 sts from start of neck
shaping to cast on edge.
Row 1: (K3, P3) 11,12,13 times, K3.
Row 2: (P3, K3) 11,12,13 times, P3.
Row 3: As row 1.

Row 4: (K3, P3) 11,12,13 times, K3.
Row 5: (P3, K3) 11,12,13 times, P3.
Row 6: As row 4.
Work rows 1 to 3 once more.
Cast off in patt.

Buttonhole band

With RS of right front facing and using 3 ¼ mm (US 3) needles pick up and knit 69,75,81 sts from cast on edge to start of neck shaping.
Work as for buttonband, working buttonholes on row 5 as folls:
Row 5 (buttonholes): (patt 1, yo, patt 2tog, patt 8,9) 6 times, patt 1, yo, patt 2tog, patt to end.

Collar

Using 3 ¼ mm (US 3) needles.
Cast on 63,69,75 sts.
Row 1: (K3, P3) 10,11,12 times, K3.
Row 2: (P3, K3) 10,11,12 times, P3.
Row 3: As row 1.
Row 4: (K3, P3) 10,11,12 times, K3.
Row 5: (P3, K3) 10,11,12 times, P3.
Row 6: As row 4.
Work these 6 rows 3 times more.
Cast off in patt.

Join both shoulder seams using backstitch.
Sew cast-on edge of collar half way across front bands.
Complete as instructed on page 48.
Sew on buttons to correspond with buttonholes.
Using oddments of yarn and Lazy Daisy stitch embroider flowers and leaves into textured diamonds as indicated in photo.

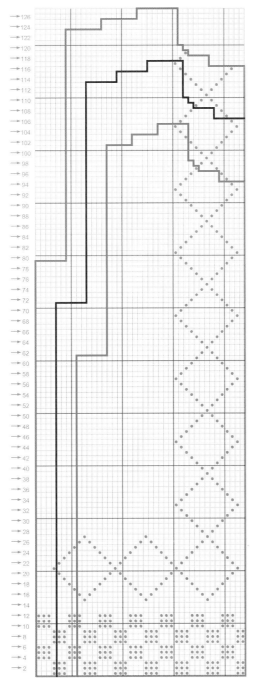

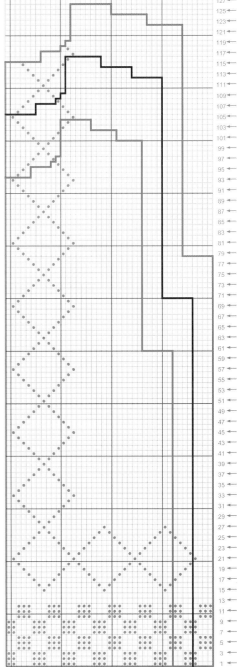

☐ K on RS
P on WS

● P on RS
K on WS

Rat tat tat Jacket

Age 1-2 years   2-3 years   3-4 years

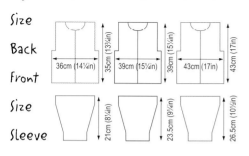

Size

Back

Front

Size

Sleeve

Yarn
Rowan All Seasons Cotton x 50g balls
Fern   6   7   7
Oddment of yarn for blanket stitch

Needles
1 pair 4 mm (US 6) needles for edging
1 pair 5 mm (US 8) needles for main body

Buttons 5

Tension
17 sts and 24 rows to 10 cm measured over stocking stitch using 5 mm (US 8) needles

Back
Using 4 mm (US 6) needles cast on 61,67,73 sts and work from chart and written instructions as folls:
Chart row 1: Knit.
Chart row 2: Knit.
Cont in garter st until chart row 10 completed.
Change to 5 mm (US 8) needles and work in stocking stitch only until chart row 52,60,68 completed.
Shape armhole

Cast off 5 sts at the beg next 2 rows. (51,57,63 sts)
Work until chart row 84,94,104 completed.
Shape shoulders and back neck
Chart row 85,95,105: K17,19,21 sts, turn and leave rem sts on a holder.
Chart row 86,96,106: Cast off 3 sts, purl to end.
Slip rem 14,16,18 sts onto a holder.
Rejoin yarn to rem sts, cast off centre 17,19,21 sts, knit to end. (17,19,21 sts)
Work 1 row
Chart row 87,97,107: Cast off 3 sts, knit to end.
Slip rem 14,16,18 sts onto a holder.

Front Pocket Linings (work 2)
Using 5 mm (US 8) needles cast on 18 sts and beg with a K row work 20,22,24 rows in st st.
Leave sts on a holder.

Left Front
Using 4 mm (US 6) needles cast on 29,32,35 sts and work from chart and written instructions as folls:
Chart row 1: Knit.
Chart row 2: Knit.
Cont in garter st until chart row 10 completed.
Change to 5 mm (US 8) needles and work as for back until chart row 30,32,34 completed.
Chart row 31,33,35 (place pocket): K6,9,11 sts, slip next 18 sts onto a holder, knit across 18 sts from first pocket lining, knit to end.
Cont to work until row 52,60,68 completed.
Shape armhole
Cast off 5 sts at the beg next row, knit to end. (24,27,30 sts)
Work without further shaping until chart row 77,87,97 completed.
Shape front neck
Chart row 78,88,98: Cast off 4,5,6 sts, purl to end. (20,22,24 sts)
Work 1 row.
Chart row 80,90,100: Cast off 4 sts beg next row, purl to end.
Dec 1 st at neck edge on next 2 rows. (14,16,18 sts)
Work without further shaping until chart row 86,96,106 completed.
Slip rem sts onto a holder.

Right Front
Using 4 mm (US 6) needles and yarn A cast on 29,32,35 sts and work from chart and follow written instructions as folls:
Chart row 1: Knit.
Chart row 2: Knit.

Cont in garter st until chart row 10 completed.
Change to 5 mm (US 8) needles and complete to match left front, foll chart for right front and reversing shaping and placing of pocket.

Sleeves (both alike)
Using 4 mm (US 6) needles cast on 33,35,37 sts and work from chart and written instructions as folls:
Chart row 1: Knit.
Chart row 2: Knit.
Cont in garter st until chart row 10 completed.
Change to 5 mm (US 8) needles and work in stocking stitch only.
Chart row 11: Inc into first st, knit to last st, inc in last st. (35,37,39 sts)
Chart row 12: Purl.
Cont from chart, shaping sides by inc as indicated to 47,51,55 sts.
Work without further shaping until chart row 52,58,66 completed. Cast off.

Press all pieces as instructed on page 48.

Buttonband
With RS of right front facing and using 4 mm (US 6) needles pick up and knit 54,62,70 sts from cast-on edge to start of neck shaping.
Work 6 rows in garter st. Cast off knitwise.

Buttonhole band
With RS of left front facing and using 4 mm (US 6) needles pick up and knit 54,62,70 sts from start of neck shaping cast-on edge.
Work as for buttonband, working buttonholes on row 3 as folls:
Row 3 (buttonholes): K2, (yo, K2tog, K10,12,14) 4 times, yo, K2tog, K2.

Collar
Using 4 mm (US 6) needles cast on 55,59,63 sts.
Work 21,23,25 rows in garter st, ending with a RS row.
Cast off knitwise.
Join both shoulder seams using backstitch.
Sew cast-on edge of collar to neck edge, matching row ends halfway across front bands.

Pocket tops (both alike)
With RS facing slip 18 sts left on pocket holder onto 4mm (US 6) needle.
Rejoin yarn, work 5 rows in garter st ending with a RS row. Cast off knitwise.
Complete jacket as instructed on page 48.

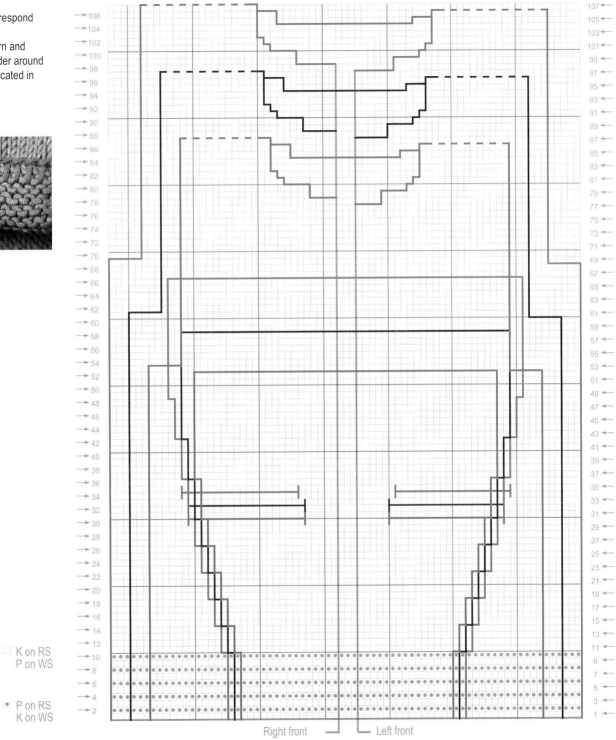

on buttons to correspond
buttonholes.
oddments of yarn and
ket stitch, embroider around
es of jacket as indicated in
to.

▢	K on RS P on WS
◉	P on RS K on WS

Right front   Left front

39

Flower Beat Sweater

Age 1-2 years 2-3 years 3-4 years

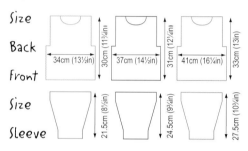

Size

Back

34cm (13½in) 30cm (11½in) 37cm (14½in) 31cm (12¼in) 41cm (16¼in) 33cm (13in)

Front

Size

Sleeve

21.5cm (8½in) 24.5cm (9¾in) 27.5cm (10¾in)

Yarn
Rowan 4 Ply cotton x 50g balls
Bloom   3   4   4
Oddments of yarn for flowers

Needles
1 pair 2 ¼ mm (US 1) needles for edging
1 pair 3 mm (US 2/3) needles for main body

Buttons 4

Tension
28 sts and 38 rows to 10cm measured over stocking stitch using 3 mm (US 2/3) needles

Back
Small edging
Using 2 ¼ mm (US 1) needles cast on 40,45,50 sts and work from chart and written instructions as folls:
Chart Row 1: Knit.
Chart Row 2: Knit.
Cont in garter st until chart row 28 completed.
Leave sts on a holder.
Large edging

Using 2 ¼ mm (US 1) needles cast on 54,59,64 sts and work from chart and written instructions as folls:
Chart Row 1: Knit.
Chart Row 2: Knit.
Cont in garter st until chart row 28 completed.
Leave sts on a holder.
Chart row 29: Knit across 40,45,50 sts from holder for small edging, then knit across 54,59,64 sts from holder for large edging.
(94,104,114 sts)
Change to 3 mm (US 2/3) needles and work in st st until chart row 78,78,82 completed.
Shape armhole
Cast off 7 sts at the beg next 2 rows.
(80,90,100 sts)
Work until chart row 128,132,140 completed.
Shape shoulders and back neck
Cast off 6,7,9 sts at the beg next 2 rows.
Chart row 131,135,143: Cast off 6,7,9 sts, knit until 9,11,11 sts on RH needle, turn and leave rem sts on a holder.
Chart row 132,136,144: Cast off 3 sts, purl to end.
Cast off rem 6,8,8 sts.
Slip centre 38,40,42 sts onto a holder, rejoin yarn to rem sts and knit to end.
(15,18,20 sts)
Chart row 132,136,144: Cast off 6,7,9 sts, purl to end.
(9,11,11 sts)
Chart row 133,137,145: Cast off 3 sts, knit to end.
Cast off rem 6,8,8 sts.

Front
Work as for back until chart row 118,122,130 completed.
Shape front neck
Chart row 119,123,131: Knit 26,30,34 sts, turn and leave rem sts on a holder.
Chart row 120,124,132: Cast off 4 sts, purl to end.
Dec 1 st at neck edge on next 4 rows. (18,22,26 sts)
Work without further shaping until chart row 128,132,140 completed.
Cast off 6,7,9 sts at beg next row and foll alt row.
Work 1 row.
Cast off rem 6,8,8, sts.
Slip centre 28,30,32 sts onto a holder, rejoin yarn to rem sts and knit to end. (26,30,34 sts)
Chart row 120,124,132: Purl 1 row.
Chart row 121,125,133: Cast off 4 sts, knit to end.
Dec 1 st at neck edge on next 4 rows. (18,22,26 sts)
Work without further shaping until chart row 129,133,141 completed.
Cast off 6,7,9 sts at beg next row and foll alt row.

Work 1 row.
Cast off rem 6,8,8, sts.

Sleeves (both alike)
Using 2 ¼ mm (US 1) needles cast on 48,50,52 sts work from written instructions as folls:
Chart Row 1: Knit.
Chart Row 2: Knit.
Cont in garter st until chart row 30 completed.
Change to 3 mm (US 2/3) needles and work in st st from chart.
Chart row 31: Inc into first st, knit to last st, inc into last st. (50,52,54 sts)
Chart row 32: Purl.
Cont from chart, shaping sides by inc as indicated to 72,78,84 sts.
Work without further shaping until chart row 96,108,118 completed.
Cast off.

Press all pieces as instructed on page 48.

Neckband
Join right shoulder using backstitch.
Using 2 ¼ mm (US 1) needles pick up and knit 16 sts down left front neck, knit across 28,30,32 sts from holder, pick up and knit 16 sts to shoulder and 3 sts down right back neck, knit across 38,40,42 sts from holder and pick up and knit 3 sts to shoulder. (104,108,112 sts)
Work 6 rows in garter st.
Cast off knitwise.
Join left shoulder and neck edging using back stitch.

Flowers (garment photographed has 4)
Using 3 mm (US2/3) needles and contrast colour 1 cast on 62 sts using the thumb method.
Row 1: Knit.
Change to contrast colour 2.
Row 2: K1, [(yo,K1) twice, (K2tog) 4 times, (yo,K1) twice] 5 times, K1.
Row 3: K1, purl to last st, K1.
Row 4 (dec): K1, (yo, K2, (K2tog) 4 times,K1,yo,K1) 5 times, K1. (52 sts)
Row 5: K1, purl to last st, K1.
Row 6 (dec): K1, K2tog to last st, K1. (27 sts)
Row 7: K1, purl to last st, K1.
Row 8 (dec): K1, K2tog to last 2 sts, K2. (15 sts)
Stitch the flower together using backstitch. Sew 1 flower to garment at split for bottom edgings on sweater front and back. Sew 2 flowers as a corsage on sweater front. Sew button at centre of each flower

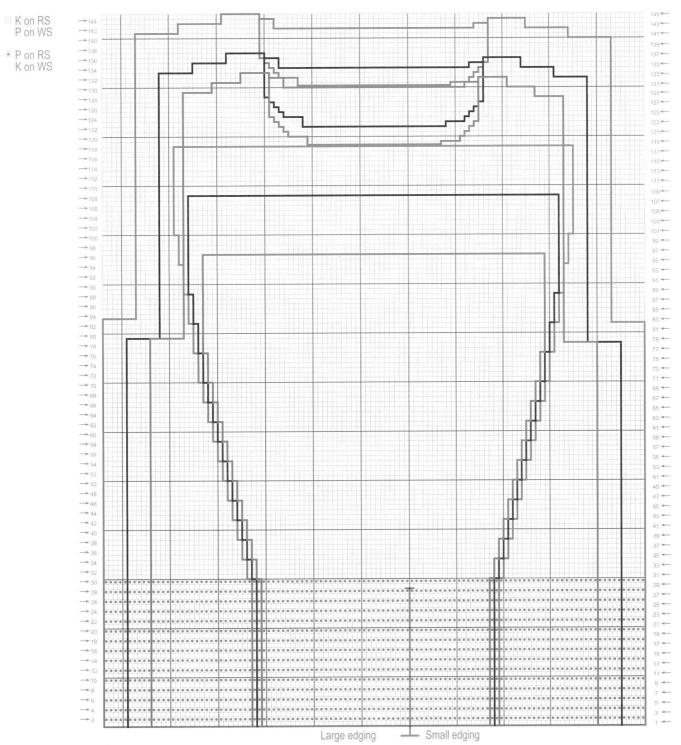

K on RS
P on WS

P on RS
K on WS

Large edging · Small edging

41

Plink Plonk Sweater

Age 1-2 years 2-3 years 3-4 years

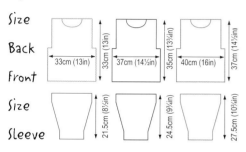

Size Back Front

33cm (13in) (13in) 37cm (14½in) (13in) 35cm (13¾in) 40cm (16in) (14¼in)

Size Sleeve

21.5cm (8½in) 24.5cm (9¾in) 27.5cm (10¾in)

Yarn
Rowan Wool Cotton x 50g balls
Navy   5   5   6

Needles
1 pair 3 ¼ mm (US 3) needles for edging
1 pair 4 mm (US 6) needles for main body

Tension
22 sts and 30 rows to 10 cm measured over stitch
stitch using 4 mm (US 6) needles

Back
Using 3 ¼ mm (US 3) needles cast on 73,81,89 sts and
work from chart and written instructions as folls:
Chart row 1: Knit.
Chart row 2: Purl.
Cont in st st from chart until row 9 completed
Chart row 10: Knit.
Chart row 11: (K1, P1) to last st, K1.
Chart row 12: (K1, P1) to last st, K1.
Cont in moss st from chart until row 20 completed
Change to 4 mm (US 6) needles work from chart until
row 72,76,80 completed.

Shape armhole
Cast off 6 sts at the beg next 2 rows.
(61,69,77 sts)
Work until chart row 110,116,122 completed.
Shape shoulders and back neck
Chart row 111,117,123: Knit 18,21,24 sts, turn and
leave rem sts on a holder.
Chart row 112,118,124: Cast off 3 sts, purl to end.
Slip rem 15,18,21 sts onto a holder.
Rejoin yarn to rem sts, cast off centre 25,27,29 sts,
knit to end. (18,21,24 sts)
Work 1 row.
Chart row 113,119,125: Cast off 3 sts, knit to end.
Slip rem 15,18,21 sts onto a holder.

Front
Work as for back until chart row 14 completed.
Chart row 15: (K1, P1) 16,18,20 times, K1, P2tog tbl,
yo, P1, K1, P1, yo, P2tog, (K1, P1) to last st, K1.
Cont in moss st from chart until row 20 completed
Cont as for back until chart row 72,76,80 completed.
Shape armholes and front neck
Chart row 73,77,81: Cast off 6 sts, Knit until 28,32,36
sts on RH needle, turn and leave rem sts on a holder.
Work 5 rows in st st.
Chart row 79,83,87: Knit 24,28,32 sts, K2tog tbl, K2.
(27,31,35 sts)
Working all decs as set by last row, cont to dec at
neck edge as indicated to 24,28,32sts. Work without
further shaping until chart row 101,107,113 completed.
Chart row 102,108,114: cast off 5,6,7 sts, purl to end.
(19,22,25 sts)
Dec 1 st at neck edge on next 4 rows.
(15,18,21 sts)
Work until chart row 112,118,124 completed.
Slip rem sts onto a holder.
Rejoin yarn to rem sts, cast off centre 5 sts,
knit to end.
Shape armhole
Chart row 74,78,82: Cast off 6 sts, purl to end
(28,32,36 sts)
Work 4 rows in st st.
Chart row 79,83,87: K2, K2tog, knit to end.
Working all decs as set by last row, cont to dec at
neck edge as indicated to 24,28,32 sts. Work without
further shaping until chart row 102,108,114 completed.
Chart row 103,109,115: cast off 5,6,7 sts, knit to end.
(19,22,25 sts)
Dec 1 st at neck edge on next 4 rows.
(15,18,21 sts)
Work until chart row 113,119,125 completed.
Slip rem sts onto a holder.

Sleeves (both alike)
Using 3 ¼ mm (US 3) needles cast on 35,37,39 sts
and work from chart starting at row 10 and written
instructions as folls:
Chart row 11: K0,1,0, (P1, K1) to last 1,0,1 st, P1,0,1
Chart row 12: K0,1,0, (P1, K1) to last 1,0,1 st, P1,0,1
Cont in moss st from chart until row 20 (10 rows
moss st) completed
Change to 4 mm (US 6) needles.
Chart row 21: Inc into first st, knit to last st, inc into
last st. (37,39,41 sts)
Chart row 22: Purl.
Cont in st st **at the same time** shape sides by inc as
indicated to 57,61,65 sts.
Work without further shaping until chart row 76,86,9
completed.
Cast off.

Press all pieces as shown in making up instructions
page 48.
Join both shoulder seams by knitting sts together on
the RS of garment.

Right Front neck edging
With RS of right front facing and using 3 ¼ mm
(US 3) needles pick up and knit 24,26,28 sts from ca
off centre front sts to start of neck shaping.
Row 1 (WS row): K1,P1 to end
Row 2: P1, K1 to end
Eyelet row (RS row): Patt 3,2,3, (K2tog, yo,
patt 2,3,3) 4 times, K2tog, yo, patt 3,2,3
Work 2 more rows in moss st.
Cast off in patt.

Left Front neck edgeing
With RS of left front facing and using 3 ¼ mm (US 3)
needles pick up and knit 24,26,28 sts from start of
neck shaping to cast off sts at centre front neck.
Work as right front edging

Neckband
With RS facing and using 3 ¼ mm (US 3) needles pic
up and knit 5 sts across right front edging, 15,16,17 st
up right front neck shaping, 31,33,35 sts across back
neck, and 15,16,17 sts down left front neck, and 5 sts
from left front edging. (71,75,79 sts)
Row 1 (WS row): (K1, P1) to last st, K1.
Row 2: (K1, P1) to last st, K1.
Buttonhole row (RS row): Patt 3, K2tog, yo, patt to
last 5 sts, K2tog, yo, patt 3.
Work 2 more rows in moss st.
Cast off in patt.

king up
garment hem to wrong side
secure with slip st. Slip stitch
place left front edging to cast
sts at front neck. Slip stitch into
ce right front edging to cast off
behind left front edging. Make 2
gths of twisted cord as explained
page 27.

ead 1st length through hem and
ure with a knot, adjust length of
d. Thread 2nd length through
eyelets in front neck edging as
strated in photograph of garment.

☐ K on RS
P on WS

• P on RS
K on WS

○ Yarn over

☒ K2tog

☒ K2tog tbl

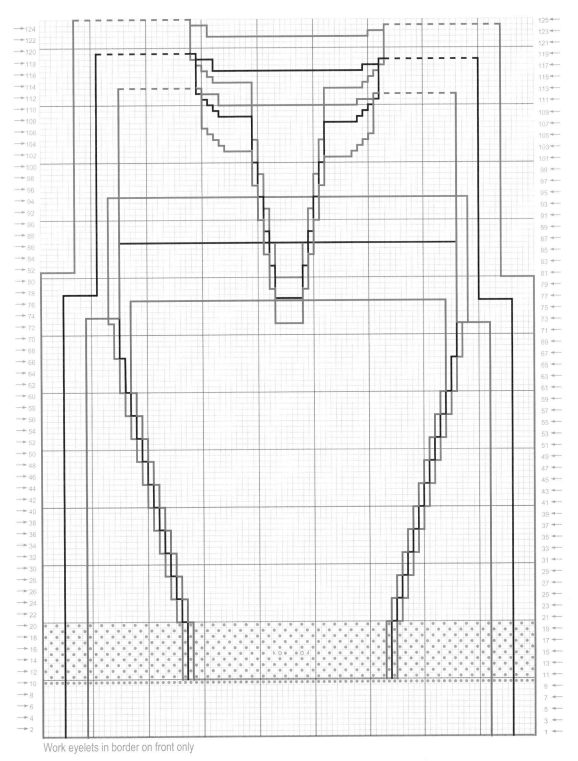

Work eyelets in border on front only

43

Ribbon Melody Cardigan

Age 1-2 years   2-3 years   3-4 years

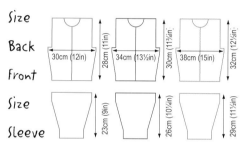

Yarn
Rowan 4 ply Cotton x 50g balls
Bluebell   3   4   4

Needles
1 pair 2 ¼ mm (US 1) needles for edging
1 pair 3 mm (US 2/3) needles for main body

Buttons 5

Ribbon 2 metres x 2.5mm wide

Tension
28 sts and 38 rows to 10 cm measured over st st using 3 mm (US 2/3) needles

Note Eyelets at centre are worked on cardigan fronts only

Back
Using 2 ¼ mm (US 1) needles cast on 77,87,97 sts and work from chart and written instructions as folls:
Chart row 1: K1,0,1, (P1, K1) to last 0,1,0 sts, P0,1,0.
Chart row 2: K1,0,1, (P1, K1) to last 0,1,0 sts, P0,1,0.

These 2 rows form moss st, work until chart row 8 completed.
Change to 3 mm (US 2/3) needles and work 2 rows in st st from chart.
Chart row 11: K3,4,1, (K2tog tbl, yo, K2) 9,10,12 times, (K1, yo, K2tog, K1) 9,10,12 times, K2,3,0.
Chart row 12: Purl
Cont in st st until chart row 16 completed.
Chart row 17: Inc into first st, knit to last st, inc into last st. (79,89,99 sts)
Cont from chart shaping sides by inc as indicated to 85,95,105 sts.
Work without further shaping until chart row 58,62,66 completed.
Shape armhole
Cast off 7 sts at the beg next 2 rows. (71,81,91 sts)
Work until chart row 108,116,124 completed.
Shape shoulders and back neck
Cast off 6,8,9 sts at the beg next 2 rows.
Chart row 111,119,127: Cast off 6,8,9 sts, knit until 10,10,12 sts on RH needle, turn and leave rem sts on a holder.
Chart row 112,120,128: Cast off 3 sts, purl to end. Cast off rem 7,7,9 sts.
Rejoin yarn and cast off centre 27,29,31 sts, knit to end. (16,18,21 sts)
Chart row 112,120,128: Cast off 6,8,9 sts, purl to end. (10,10,12 sts)
Chart row 113,121,129: Cast off 3 sts, knit to end. Cast off rem 7,7,9 sts.

Left Front
Using 2 ¼ mm (US 1) needles cast on 36,41,46 sts and work from chart and written instructions as folls:
Chart row 1: K1,0,1, (P1, K1) to last st, P1.
Chart row 2: (P1, K1) to last 0,1,0 sts, P0,1,0.
These 2 rows form moss st, work until chart row 8 completed.
Change to 3 mm (US 2/3) needles and work 2 rows in st st from chart.
Chart row 11: K3,4,1, (K2tog tbl, yo, K2) 8,9,11 times, K1.
Chart row 12: Purl
Cont in st st until chart row 16 completed.
Chart row 17: Inc into first st, knit to last 5 sts, K2tog tbl, yo K3. (37,42,47 sts)
Cont from chart, working eyelets as above on every 6th row, and inc at side edge as indicated to 40,45,50 sts. Work without further shaping until chart row 58,62,66 completed.
Shape armhole
Cast off 7 sts at the beg next 2 rows. (33,38,43 sts)

Work until chart row 99,107,115 completed.
Shape front neck
Cast off 6,7,8 sts at the beg next row.
Work 1 row.
Chart row 102,110,118: Cast off 4 sts, purl to end.
Dec 1 st at neck edge on next 4 rows. (19,23,27 sts)
Work until chart row 108,116,124 completed.
Shape shoulder
Cast off 6,8,9 sts at the beg next row and foll alt row
Work 1 row
Cast off rem 7,7,9 sts.

Right Front
Using 2 ¼ mm (US 1) needles cast on 36,41,46 sts and work from chart and written instructions as folls:
Chart row 1: (P1, K1) to last 0,1,0 sts, P0,1,0.
Chart row 2: K1,0,1, (P1, K1) to last st, P1.
These 2 rows form moss st, work until chart row 8 completed.
Change to 3 mm (US 2/3) needles and work 2 rows in st st from chart.
Chart row 11: K2, (K1, yo, K2tog K1) 8,9,11 times, K2,3,0.
Chart row 12: Purl
Cont in st st until chart row 16 completed.
Chart row 17: K3, yo, K2tog, K to last st, inc in last st
Cont from chart, placing eyelets on every 6th row and working incs as indicated.
Complete to match left front, foll chart for right front and reversing shaping.

Sleeves (both alike)
Using 2 ¼ mm (US 1) needles cast on 45,47,49 sts and work from chart and written instructions as folls:
Chart row 1: K1,0,1, (P1, K1) to last 0,1,0 sts, P0,1,0.
Chart row 2: K1,0,1, (P1, K1) to last 0,1,0 sts, P0,1,0.
These 2 rows form moss st, work until chart row 8 completed.
Change to 3 mm (US 2/3) needles.
Chart row 9: Inc into first st, knit to last st, inc into last st. (47,49,51 sts)
Chart row 10: Purl to end.
Chart row 11: K4,1,2 (K2tog tbl, yo, K2) 5,6,6 times, (K1, yo, K2tog, K1) 5,6,6 times, K3,0,1.
Chart row 12: Purl
Cont from chart, shaping sides by inc as indicated to 73,79,85 sts.
Work without further shaping until chart row 90,100,11 completed.
Cast off.

Press all pieces as instructed on page 48.

tonhole band

RS of right front facing and using
mm (US 1) needles pick up and
79,83,87 sts from cast-on edge to
t of neck shaping.

v 1 (WS row): K1, P1 to last st, K1
v 2: as row 1
v 3 (buttonholes): (Patt 17,18,19,
2tog, yo,) 4 times, patt 3
k 3 more rows in moss st.
t off knitwise on WS.

ttonband

h RS of left front facing and using
mm (US 1) needles pick up and
79,83,87 sts from start of neck
ping to cast-on edge.
rk 6 rows in moss st.
t off knitwise on WS.

ckband

both shoulder seams using
kstitch.
h RS facing and using 2 ¼ mm
1) needles pick up and knit 5 sts
oss buttonhole band, 20,21,22 sts up
t front neck shaping,
35,37 sts across back neck, and
21,22 sts down left front neck, and 5
from buttonband. (83,87,91 sts)
v 1 (WS row): K1, P1 to last st, K1
v 2: as row 1
v 3 (buttonholes): Patt to last 5 sts,
t 2tog, yo, patt to end.
rk 3 more rows in moss st.
t off knitwise on WS.

mplete cardigan as instructed on
ge 48.
w on buttons to correspond with
ttonholes.
rting at right front neck thread
oon through eyelets on garment
nts and back as in garment
otograph. Starting at centre eyelets
sleeve, thread ribbon through
elets, bring ribbon back to centre, tie
mall bow, secure with a few stitches.

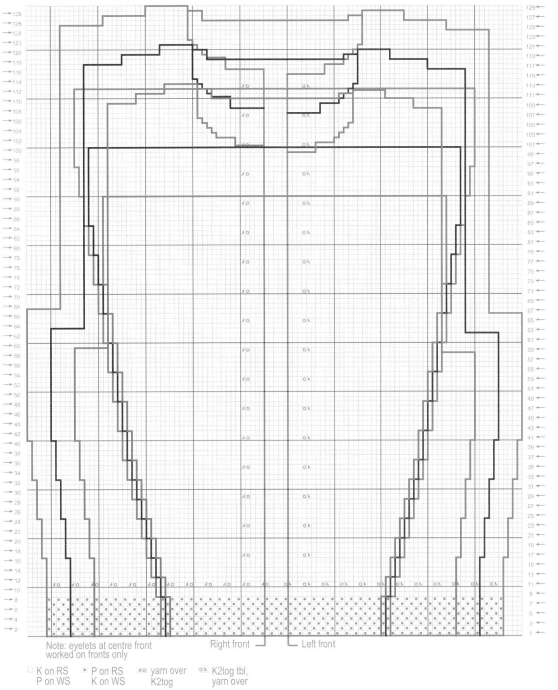

Note: eyelets at centre front
worked on fronts only

Right front ⌐   ⌐ Left front

☐ K on RS   • P on RS   ⚹⊙ yarn over   ⊙⚹ K2tog tbl,
   P on WS   K on WS   K2tog   yarn over

The Blues Slipover

Age 1-2 years 2-3 years 3-4 years

Size

Back

Front

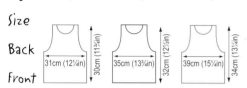

31cm (12¼in) 30cm (11¾in)
35cm (13¾in) 32cm (12½in)
39cm (15¼in) 34cm (13¼in)

Yarn

Rowan Handknit Cotton x 50g balls

A. Navy	1	2	2
B. Ice Water	2	2	2
C. Grey	2	2	2

Needles

1 pair 3 ¼ mm (US 3) needles for edging
1 pair 4 mm (US 6) needles for main body

Tension

20 sts and 28 rows to 10 cm measured over patterned stocking stitch using 4 mm (US 6) needles.

Back

Using 3 ¼ mm (US 3) needles and yarn A, cast on 61,69,77 sts and work from chart and written instructions as folls:
Chart row 1: K2,1,0, (P2, K3) 11,13,15 times, P2, K2,1,0.
Chart row 2: P2,1,0 (K2, P3) 11,13,15 times, K2, P2,1,0.
Cont in rib from chart until row 10 completed
Change to 4 mm (US 6) needles and joining in and breaking off colours as indicated on chart work in patterned stocking stitch using the intarsia technique for each block of colour, work until chart row 50,54,58 completed.

Shape armhole

Cast off 4 sts at beginning next 2 rows. (53,61,69 sts)
Dec 1 st at each end of next 3 rows and 2 foll alt rows. (43,51,59 sts)
Work 3 rows in patt.
Dec 1 st at each end of next row. (41,49,57 sts)
Work without further shaping to chart row 86,92,98 completed.

Shape shoulders and back neck

Cast off 3,5,6 sts at the beg next row, patt until 6,7,9 sts on RH needle, turn and leave rem sts on a holder.
Chart row 88,94,100: Cast off 3 sts, patt to cnd.
Cast off rem 3,4,6 sts.
Slip centre 23,25,27 sts onto a holder, rejoin yarn to rem sts and patt to end. (9,12,15 sts)
Chart row 88,94,100: Cast off 3,5,6 sts, patt to end. (6,7,9 sts)
Chart row 89,95,101: Cast off 3 sts, patt to end.
Cast off rem 3,4,6 sts.

Front

Work as for back until chart row 80,86,92 completed.
Shape front neck
Chart row 81,87,93: K12,15,18 sts, turn and leave rem sts on a holder.
Chart row 82,88,94: Cast off 4 sts, patt to end.
Dec 1 st at neck edge on next 2 rows. (6,9,12 sts)
Work without further shaping until chart row 86,92,98 completed.
Cast off 3,5,6 sts at beg next row.
Work 1 row.
Cast off rem 3,4,6 sts.
Slip centre 17,19,21 sts onto a holder, rejoin yarn to rem sts and patt to end. (12,15,18 sts)
Work 1 row.
Chart row 83,89,95: Cast off 4 sts, patt to end.
Dec 1 st at neck edge on next 2 rows. (6,9,12 sts)
Work without further shaping until chart row 87,93,99 completed
Shape shoulder
Cast off 3,5,6 sts at beg next row.
Work 1 row.
Cast off rem 3,4,6 sts.

Press all pieces as instructed on page 48.
As explained on page 27, and using yarn A Swiss darn in a grid pattern through the centre of each colour block horizontally and vertically as illustrated opposite.
Join right shoulder seam using backstitch.

Neck Edging

With RS facing and using 3 ¼ mm (US 3) needles and yarn A pick up and knit 10 sts down left front neck, knit across 17,19,21, sts from front neck holder, pick up and knit 10 sts to shoulder and 3 sts down right back neck, knit across 23,25,27 sts from back neck holder, pick up and knit 3 sts to shoulder. (66,70,74 sts)
Chart row 1: K2,2,1, (P2, K3) 12,13,14 times, P2, K2,1,1.
Chart row 2: P2,1,1, (K2, P3) 12,13,14 times, K2, P2,2,1.
Work 6 more rows in rib as sts set.
Cast off in rib.
Join left shoulder seam using backstitch.

Armhole edging (both alike)

With RS facing and using 3 ¼ mm (US 3) needles and yarn A pick up and knit 30,32,34 sts from side seam to shoulder and 30,32,34 sts down to side sea (60,64,68 sts)
Knit 2 rows.
Cast off knitwise.

Complete slipover as instructed on page 48.

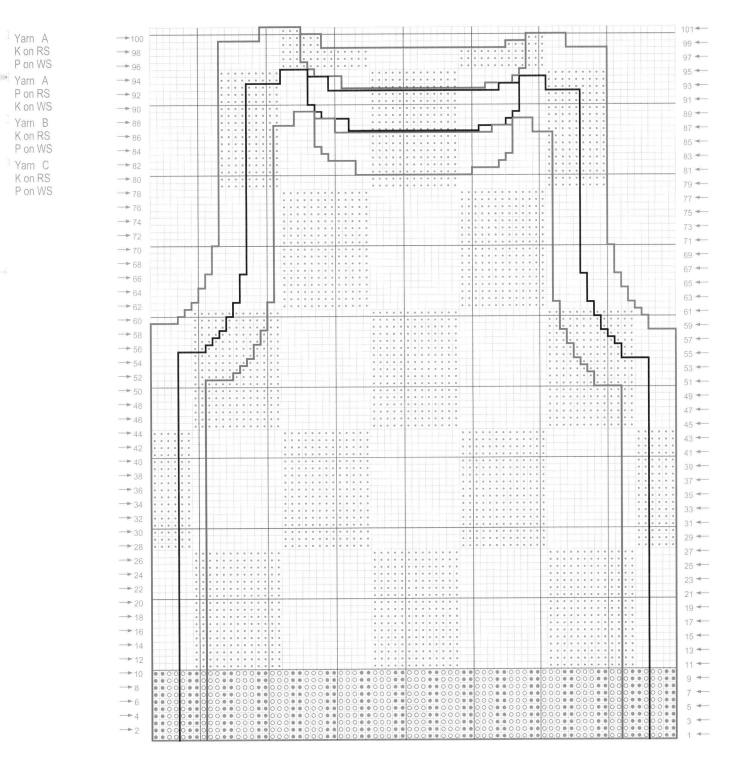

47

Knitting Techniques
A simple guide to making up and finishing

Putting your garment together

After spending many hours knitting it is essential that you complete your garment correctly. Following the written instructions, and illustrations we show you how easy it is to achieve a beautifully finished garment which will withstand the most boisterous child!

Pressing

With the wrong side of the fabric facing, pin out each knitted garment piece onto an ironing board using the measurements given in the size diagram. As each yarn is different, refer to the ball band and press pieces according to instructions given. Pressing the knitted fabric will help the pieces maintain their shape and give a smooth finish.

Sewing in ends

Once you have pressed your finished pieces, sew in all loose ends. Thread a darning needle with yarn, weave needle along approx 5 sts on wrong side of fabric; pull thread through. Weave needle in opposite direction approx 5 sts; pull thread through, cut end of yarn.

Making Up

If you are making a sweater join the right shoulder seam as instructed in the pattern, now work the neck edging. Join left shoulder seam and neck edging. If you are making a cardigan, join both shoulder seams as in the pattern and work edgings as instructed. Sew on buttons to correspond with buttonholes. Insert square set in sleeves as follows: Sew cast off edge of sleeve top into armhole. Making a neat right angle, sew in the straight sides at top of sleeve to cast off stitches at armhole. Join side and sleeve seams using either mattress stitch or back stitch. It is important to press each of the seams as you make the garment up.

Casting Off shoulder Seams together

This method secures the front and back shoulder stitches together, it also creates a small ridged seam. It is important that the cast off edge should be elastic like the rest of the fabric; if you find that your cast off is too tight, try using a larger needle. You can cast off with the seam on the right side (as illustrated) or wrong side of garment.

1. Place wrong sides of fabric together. Hold both needles with the stitches on in LH, insert RH needle into first stitch on both LH needles.

2. Draw the RH needle through both stitches.

3. Making one stitch on RH needle.

4. Knit the next stitch from both LH needles, two stitches on RH needle.

5. Using the point of one needle in LH, insert into first stitch on RH needle. Take the first stitch over the second stitch.

6. Repeat from 4. until one stitch left on right hand needle. Cut yarn and draw cut end through stitch to secure.

Picking Up Stitches

Once you have finished all the garment pieces, pressed them and sewn in all ends, you need to complete the garment by adding a neckband, front bands, or armhole edgings. This is done by picking up stitches along the edge of the knitted piece. The number of stitches to pick up is given in the pattern; these are made using a new yarn. When you pick up horizontally along a row of knitting it is important that you pick up through a whole stitch. When picking up stitches along a row edge, pick up one stitch in from the edge, this gives a neat professional finish.

1. Holding work in LH, with RS of fabric facing, insert RH needle into a whole stitch below the cast off edge, wrap new yarn around needle.

2. Draw the RH needle through fabric, making a loop with new yarn on right hand needle.

3. Repeat this action into the next stitch following the pattern instructions until all stitches have been picked up.

4. Work edging as instructed.

Mattress Stitch

This method of sewing up is worked on the right side of the fabric and is ideal for matching stripes. Mattress stitch should be worked one stitch in from edge to give the best finish. With RS of work facing, lay the two pieces to be joined edge to edge. Insert needle from WS between edge st and second st. Take yarn to opposite piece, insert needle from front, pass the needle under two rows, bring it back through to the front.

1. Work mattress stitch foundation as above.

2. Return yarn to opposite side working under two rows at a time, repeat.

3. At regular intervals gently pull stitches together.

4. The finished seam is very neat and almost impossible to see.

Back Stitch

This method of sewing up is ideal for shoulder and armhole seams as it does not allow the fabric to stretch out of shape. Pin the pieces with right sides together. Insert needle into fabric at end, one stitch or row from edge, take the needle round the two edges securing them. Insert needle into fabric just behind where last stitch came out and make a short stitch . Re-insert needle where previous stitch started, bring up needle to make a longer stitch. Re-insert needle where last stitch ended. Repeat to end, taking care to match any pattern.

Sewing in a Zip

With right side facing, neatly match row ends and slip stitch fronts of garment together. Pin zip into place, with right side of zip to wrong side of garment, matching centre front of garment to centre of zip. Neatly backstitch into place using a matching coloured thread. Undo slip stitches. Zip inserted.

Rowan Overseas Distributors

AUSTRALIA : Australian Country Spinners, 314 Albert Street, Brunswick, Victoria 3056. Tel : (03) 9380 3888

BELGIUM : Pavan, Meerlaanstraat 73, B9860 Balegem (Oosterzele). Tel : (32) 9 221 8594
Email : pavan@pandora.be

CANADA : Diamond Yarn, 9697 St Laurent, Montreal, Quebec, H3L 2N1. Tel :(514) 388 6188
Diamond Yarn (Toronto), 155 Martin Ross, Unit 3, Toronto, Ontario, M3J 2L9. Tel :(416) 736 6111
Email : diamond@diamondyarn.com URL : http://www.diamondyarn.com

DENMARK : Please contact Rowan for stockist details.

FRANCE : Elle Tricot, 8 Rue du Coq, 67000 Strasbourg. Tel : (33) 3 88 23 03 13.
Email : elletricot@agat.net

GERMANY : Wolle & Design, Wolfshovener Strasse 76, 52428 Julich-Stetternich. Tel : (49) 2461 54735.
Email : Info@wolleunddesign.de URL : http://www.wolleunddesign.de

HOLLAND : de Afstap, Oude Leliestraat 12, 1015 AW Amsterdam. Tel : (31) 20 6231445.

HONG KONG : East Unity Co Ltd, Unit B2, 7/F, Block B, Kailey Industrial Centre, 12 Fung Yip Street, Chai Wan.
Tel : (852) 2869 7110. Fax : (852) 2537 6952
Email : eastuni@netvigator.com

ICELAND : Storkurinn, Laugavegi 59,101 Reykjavik. Tel : (354) 551 8258 Fax : (354) 562 8252
Email : malin@mmedia.is

JAPAN : Puppy Co Ltd, TOC Building, 7-22-17 Nishigotanda, Shinagawa-ku, Tokyo. Tel : (81) 3 3494 2435.
Email : info@rowan-jaeger.com

KOREA : De Win Co Ltd, Chongam Bldg, 101, 34-7 Samsung-dong, Seoul.
Tel : (82) 2511 1087. E mail : dewin@dewin.co.kr. URL : http://www.dewin.co.kr

NEW ZEALAND : Please contact Rowan for stockist details.

NORWAY : Paa Pinne, Tennisvn 3D, 0777 Oslo. Tel : (47) 909 62 818.
Email : design@paapinne.no URL : http://www.paapinne.no

SWEDEN : Wincent, Norrtullsgaten 65, 113 45 Stockholm. Tel : (46) 8 33 70 60 Fax : (46) 8 33 70 68.
Email : wincent@chello.se URL : http://www.wincent.nv

TAIWAN : Green Leave, No 181, Sec 4, Chung Ching N. Road, Taipei, Taiwan R.O.C. Tel : (886) 2 8221 2925.
Chien He Wool Knitting Co, 10 -1 313 Lane, Sec 3, Cmung-Ching North Road, Taipei, Taiwan. Tel : (886) 2 2596 0269

U.S.A : Rowan USA, 4 Townsend West, Suite 8, Nashua, New Hampshire 03063. Tel : (1 603) 886 5041 / 5043.
Email : rowan@westminsterfibers.com

UNITED KINGDOM : Green Lane Mill, Holmfirth,West Yorkshire, HD9 2DX. Tel : (44) (0) 1484 681881.
Email : missbea@knitrowan.com URL : http://www.knitrowan.com